Haddon Hall

Haddon Hall

Sydney Grundy and Arthur Sullivan

MINT EDITIONS

Haddon Hall was first published in 1893.

This edition published by Mint Editions 2021.

ISBN 9781513281483 | E-ISBN 9781513286501

Published by Mint Editions®

MINT EDITIONS

minteditionbooks.com

Publishing Director: Jennifer Newens
Design & Production: Rachel Lopez Metzger
Project Manager: Micaela Clark
Typesetting: Westchester Publishing Services

"To thine own self be true,
And it must follow, as the night the day,
Thou canst not then be false to any man!"

—Shakespeare

Dramatis Personae

John Manners	}	
Sir George Vernon	}	Royalists.
Oswald	}	
Rupert Vernon (*Roundhead*)		
The McCrankie	}	
Sing-Song Simeon	}	
Kill-Joy Candlemas	}	Puritans.
Nicodemus Knock-Knee	}	
Barnabas Bellows-to-Mend	}	
Major Domo		
Dorothy Vernon		
Lady Vernon		
Dorcas		
Nance		
Gertrude		
Deborah		

Chorus of Simples and Gentles

Act I.—The Lovers.   Scene.—The Terrace.
"The green old turrets, all ivy thatch,
Above the cedars that girdle them rise,
The pleasant glow of the sunshine catch,
And outline sharp on the bluest of skies."

Act II.—The Elopement.   Scene I.—Dorothy Vernon's Door.
Scene II.—The Long Gallery
"It is a night with never a star,
And the hall with revelry throbs and gleams;
There grates a hinge—the door is ajar—
And a shaft of light in the darkness streams."

Act III.—The Return.   Scene.—The Ante-Chamber.

NOTE: The clock of Time has been put forward a century, and other liberties have been taken with history.

PROLOGUE

MEN: Ye stately homes of England,
    So simple yet so grand;
  Long may ye stand and flourish,
    Types of our English land!
WOMEN: Ye stately homes of England,
    Such mansions only grew
  Where virtue reigned from cot to throne,
    And man and wife were true.
FULL CHORUS: Ye stately homes of England,
    Long may your towers stand;
  Types of the life of man and wife,
    Types of our English land!

Act I

Scene.—*The Terrace.*

Chorus.

To-day, it is a festal time!
    The bridegroom comes to-day,
And we are here to sing a rhyme
    To speed him on his way.
To-day, our mistress, ever dear,
    Doth plight her virgin troth;
And we are all forgathered here
    To sing, God bless them both!

Dance.

Enter Dorcas.

Recitative.—Dorcas.

But midst our jubilation
    Comes the echo of a sigh;
Its full signification
    Ye will gather by-and-bye.
Now, lend me your attention
    While I tell you all a tale,
Anent a dainty dormouse
    And an unattractive snail.
Chorus: A dainty dormouse!
    An unattractive snail!

Song.—Dorcas.

'Twas a dear little dormouse—
    A little mouse-maid!
Her papa and mamma
    She had always obeyed.

Pit-a-pat went her heart,
　　And her cheek grew pale,
When commanded to marry
　　A stupid old snail.
"Oh, father, I cannot!"
　　"But, daughter, thou must;
For he has a house,
　　And we haven't a crust!"
The snail he was ugly,
　　The snail he was black;
But for all that he carried
　　A house on his back.
Said the wily old dormouse,
　　"When thou art his bride,
He will lend us his house,
　　And we'll all live inside!"
ALL: "Oh, father, I cannot!"
　　"But, daughter, thou must;
For he has a house
　　And we haven't a crust!"
DORCAS: A gallant young squirrel
　　Sat perched on a tree,
And he thought to himself,
　　There's a good wife for me!
On the eve of the wedding
　　He said to the mouse,
"Wilt thou marry a squirrel
　　Who hasn't a house?"
"Oh, squirrel, I cannot!"
　　"But, dormouse, thou must,
Her heart to a squirrel
　　A dormouse may trust."
The squirrel was handsome,
　　They plighted their vows,
And the squirrel ran off
　　With the little dormouse.
And I'm sure if you ever
　　Set eyes on a snail,
You will all sympathize

　　　　　SYDNEY GRUNDY AND ARTHUR SULLIVAN

With the dormouse's wail.
ALL: "Oh, father, I cannot!
        Don't tell me I must;
    Though he has a house
        And we haven't a crust!"
CHORUS: But who is the dormouse
    And who, who is the snail?
Enter SIR GEORGE VERNON, LADY VERNON, *and* DOROTHY.
CHORUS: Hail to the Lord of Haddon!
        And thee, his silver bride!
    And to thy daughter, fairest flower
        Of all the country side!
WOMEN: Nor violet, lily,
        Nor bluebell we bring,
    To garland thy pathway
        With fragrance of spring.
    No beauty of blossom
        That dies in a day
    Can speak an affection
        That blossoms alway.
    And never a chaplet
        Our hearts could entwine
    Could tell the devotion
        That ever is thine.
CHORUS: In lieu of the lily
        And bonny bluebell,
    We lay on thine altar
        True love's immortelles.
DOROTHY: Dear playmates of childhood,
        Right welcome are you!
    More fragrant than lily
        A love that is true.
LADY V.: Like flower amaranthine
        Whose blossoms ne'er fade,
    It blooms in the sunshine
        And blooms in the shade.
BOTH: Right welcome are you.
CHORUS: In lieu of the lily
        And bonny bluebell,

We lay on thine altar
  True love's immortelles.

Welcome, I bid ye welcome, one and all!
  Let youth and beauty keep their merry May;
For all too soon the leaves of autumn fall,
  And evening shadows quench the laughing day.

MADRIGAL.

SIR G.: When the budding bloom of May
  Paints the hedgerows red and white,
 Gather then your garlands gay;
  Earth was made for man's delight!
LADY V.: May is playtime—
DOROTHY: June is hay time—
SIR G.: Seize the day time—
TRIO: Fa la la!
  Carol now the birds of spring!
  Let our hearts in chorus sing!
CHORUS: Ere the golden day is pale,
  Dawns the silver orb of light;
 Sweetly trills the nightingale,
   "Earth was made for man's delight!"
    Fa la la!
   "Earth was made for man's delight!"
SIR G.: When the leaves of autumn sigh,
   "Nearer death and further birth!"
 Time enough for hearts to cry,
   "Man was only made for earth!"
LADY V.: Youth is pleasant—
DOROTHY: Grasp the present—
SIR G.: Moons are crescent—
TRIO: Fa la la!
   Time enough for hearts to sigh!
   Now the noonday sun is high!
CHORUS: Day in cloth of gold is gay,

Robe of silver wears the night;
All creation seems to say,
  "Earth was made for man's delight!"
    Fa la la!
  "Earth was made for man's delight!"

Exeunt Chorus and DORCAS.

SIR G.: What ails thee, Doll? This little head might hold the cares of empire. Smile on me—smile! To-day, of all days, I would have thee merry. What will our cousin Rupert think of thee?

DOROTHY: I care not what our cousin Rupert thinks.

LADY V.: Methought he liked not merriment?

SIR G.: True, Rupert hath espoused the Roundhead cause; but if I judge aright, short commons and long prayers will like not him! Be not deceived, our cousin's head is rather long than round. He serves the parliament—

LADY V.: And serves the times.

DOROTHY: In brief, he is not honest.

SIR G.: Honest, as times go. If, when he is thy husband, he is true to thee, heed not his politics.

DOROTHY: I heed them not, nor his truth either, for he will never be husband of mine.

SIR G.: Hearken, Doll. I do not care to plague thy pretty head with musty documents and lawyers' quirks; enough to say that there are some who hold our cousin's title to this fair estate stronger than ours. This marriage puts an end to doubts and questions that have troubled me, and would be grateful to the parliament, which loves me none too well.

LADY V.: Then, must Doll wed to please the parliament?

SIR G.: And me!

DOROTHY: From childhood I have striven to please thee, father.

SIR G.: And thou hast pleased me well!

DOROTHY: And I will strive to please thee still in everything save this. Do with me as thou wilt, but spare my heart. I cannot give what is not mine own.

SIR G.: Hast thou not yet forgot this youth—whose very name my lips refuse to speak?

LADY V.: Manners—John Manners.

SIR G.: Rutland's younger son! Shame on thee—shame! He is beneath thee, Doll. Remember who thou art. Remember that with thee pass all the lands of Haddon and this ancient hall, which smiles there as it smiled even before the Conquest.

DOROTHY: I know well who I am. I know from whom I am descended; nor do I forget their ancient watchword, "Drede God, and honour the King!" God I have ever dreaded; and the king I honour, by loving one whose sword hath served his cause.

SIR G.: If he would sheath that sword—if he would only pay decent respect to parliament.

DOROTHY: He were a traitor, and not worth my love! Oh, father dear, turn not from me in anger! Is it sin to love?

SIR G.: Did I speak harshly? Then forgive me, Doll! Ever since my son—my only son—died, fighting for his country, on the sea— thou art my all in all. It breaks my heart to ruffle thee. Go, tell thy lover—if he sheath his sword—if he acknowledge parliament— which otherwise might forfeit my estate—I will confer with Rupert. I can say no more.

DOROTHY: 'Twere vain to ask him. It were worse than vain.

SIR G.: It is not much I beg of thee.

DOROTHY: My lips could not affront the one I love.

SIR G.: They can affront thy father!

DOROTHY: Nay!

SIR G.: So be it! Go thy way and I go mine. Remember only that my word is given, and that a Vernon doth not break his pledge.

DOROTHY: I am a Vernon, too, and shall I not keep mine?

SIR G.: Bandy not words with me. No longer do I beg thee—I command.

TRIO.—DOROTHY, LADY VERNON, and SIR GEORGE.

DOROTHY: Nay, father dear, speak not to me
In anger's cruel tone!

LADY V.: By all the love she bears to thee—
The love that is thine own!

DOROTHY: Remember all thou art to me;
Remember all I am to thee;
And marvel not that hearts will ache—
For true love's sake!

DOROTHY and LADY V.: For true love's sake!

SIR G.: Go, bid thy lover sheath his sword

And bend his stubborn knee;
　Is all thy thought for thine adored,
　　And hast thou none for me?
LADY V.: For true love's sake a heart will sigh!
SIR G.: For true love's sake a heart will die!
DOROTHY: His oath a soldier cannot break
　For true love's sake!
DOROTHY and LADY V.: For true love's sake!

ENSEMBLE.

DOROTHY: For true love's sake a heart will break!
LADY V.: For true love's sake a heart will sigh!
SIR G.: For true love's sake a heart will die!
Exit SIR GEORGE.

DUET.—DOROTHY and LADY VERNON.

DOROTHY: Mother, dearest mother,
　　Hearken unto me,
　Think not that another
　　Draws my heart from thee.
　Though each day I know him
　　Brighter shines the sun,
　All the love I owe him
　　Robbeth thee of none.
　His I seem to borrow,
　　All mine own is thine;
　In my virgin sorrow
　　Help me, mother mine.
LADY V.: Were but I above him,
　　Simple were his task;
　Doth my daughter love him?
　　That is all I ask.
　Were but I above him,
　　Stranger though he be,
　If my daughter love him,
　　Son he is to me!
　Whether wife or maiden,

All my heart is thine;
  Joy or sorrow laden,
    Thou art daughter mine.
BOTH: Whether wife or maiden
    Thou art daughter/mother mine;
  Joy or sorrow laden,
    All my heart is thine!
DOROTHY: Mother, my own dear mother,
    Both of our lives entwine!
  Couldst thou have wed another,
    Had such a love been thine?
      Oh, mother dear,
        I love him so,
      No doubt or fear
        I seem to know!
LADY V.: Go on thy way with gladness!
    Happily live the wife!
  And leave to me the sadness,
    And leave to me the strife.
BOTH: Whether wife or maiden
    Thou art daughter/mother mine;
  Joy or sorrow laden,
    All my heart is thine!
Exeunt.
Re-enter CHORUS, *surrounding* OSWALD.
CHORUS: Ribbons to sell, ribbons to sell!
    Ribbons to tie up our hair!
  Who'll buy? I! I! and I as well!
    And now for the fun of the fair!

SONG.—OSWALD.

Come, simples and gentles, and gather ye round,
    And for your attention I'll thank'ee;
I sell by the pennyweight, pottle, and pound
    Wares English, French, German, and Yankee.
I've wares for the young, nor left out in the cold
    Are their elders, the more is the pity,
For I can't help remarking you're none of you old

And noting you're all of you pretty!
I've articles suited to every taste
    And every description of weather;
If any fair lady'll oblige with a waist,
    We'll try on this girdle together!
CHORUS: Although on his back he may carry a pack,
    He has hands of a wonderful whiteness;
And this sympathetic young peripatetic
    A paragon is of politeness!

My prices are low and my dealings are cash,
    So your pockets I won't dip in deeply;
Through buying my stock at a great London smash
    I am able to sell very cheaply;
So bid for it boldly, but please bear in mind
    That the rule of cash down is "de rigueur."
The price of each article, ladies, you'll find,
    Has been marked in a very low figure.
A complaint the proprietor bids you implore
    In case you're not treated politely,
For I am a type of a travelling store—
    In fact, I'm a premature Whitely!
CHORUS: He bought up a great metropolitan smash
    At a sacrifice truly alarming;
He doesn't deduct any discount for cash,
    But his manner is perfectly charming!

Now isn't that beautiful? isn't that nice?
    When I tell you the article's German,
You'll know it could only be sold at the price
    Through a grand international firman.
A still greater bargain! An article French.
    When I say it's of French manufacture,
I mean that if worn by a beautiful wench,
    A heart it is certain to fracture.
But here is the prize—only tuppence—pure
    gold.
    When I mention, the article's Yankee,
Well, nobody then will require to be told

That there can't be the least hanky-panky!

OSWALD: Who'll buy?

CHORUS: Not I!

OSWALD: Who'll buy?

CHORUS: Not I!

OSWALD: A chance like this you mustn't miss!

CHORUS: Oh, yes! oh, yes! the chance we'll miss!
But we've been told, alas!
That what is sold
As Yankee gold
Is sometimes Yankee brass.

Exeunt CHORUS.

OSWALD: This to thy mistress!

DORCAS (*recoiling*): By our lady, nay!

OSWALD: Thou art a comely wench, and thy face tells me thou art to be trusted.

DORCAS: But art thou to be trusted? For I do not know thee; and ere now packmen have been found deceivers.

OSWALD: I am no packman! Lo! (*Throws aside his cloak*) God save the King!

DORCAS: Grammercy! 'tis a gallant gentleman! (*Holds out her hand*) Now will I trust thee.

OSWALD: But thou dost not know me, and ere now young men have been found deceivers.

DORCAS: I'll hazard it! (OSWALD *gives her the letter*) Nay, prithee, do not cover thyself up ere I have had another glimpse of thee. (OSWALD *flings off his cloak*) (*Aside*) Truly a most desirable young man! (*Aloud*) Dost come from London, sir?

OSWALD: From London—aye!

DORCAS (*aside, clasping hands*): What pretty things they make in London town! (*Aloud*) Of course, sir, thou art some fine gentleman?

OSWALD: No—but a soldier and a serving-man.

DORCAS: A serving-man! And I a serving-maid! Then this (*indicating letter*) comes not from thee?

OSWALD: From Master Manners. He is to whom I owe suit and service.

DORCAS: From Master Manners! Then I guess its burden.

OSWALD: Carry that burden to thy mistress, straight.

DORCAS: Is there such haste?

OSWALD: My master is hard by, and he awaits an answer.

SYDNEY GRUNDY AND ARTHUR SULLIVAN

DORCAS: Look me in the face! Art thou indeed a servant? or art thou
thine own master—in disguise?

OSWALD: Nay, I am only my plain self.

DORCAS: Thank Heaven!

OSWALD: Oswald, my name!

DORCAS: Mine, Dorcas.

OSWALD: Shall we be friends?

DORCAS: With all my heart! (OSWALD *approaches her, she draws back*)
Hold! our acquaintance is too young for that.

OSWALD: For what? I did but offer thee my hand.

DORCAS: Was it thy hand?

OSWALD: I dared not offer more; but if thou challenge me——

DORCAS (*recoiling*): Not I!

OSWALD: Thou art a winsome wench, but thou art coy.

DORCAS: Thou art not coy!

OSWALD: Life is to brief for modesty (*holding her*)

DORCAS (*reflectively*): 'Tis rather waste of time.

OSWALD: We shall not long be young.

DORCAS: And in the end it comes to the same thing.

OSWALD: That is philosophy (*kisses her*)

DORCAS: Enough—for the first lesson. Art thou a great philosopher?

OSWALD: Aye; for I've read life's riddle. Life holds one secret. Live!

DUET.—DORCAS and OSWALD.

OSWALD: The sun's in the sky, and
  The grass in the ground;
    Nature maternal,
    Placid, supernal,
    Spreadeth her vernal
  Mantle around.
DORCAS: 'Tis idle repining,
  When summer is gay;
    When from her coffers
    Jewels she offers,
    Scorn not her proffers,
  Say her not nay!
OSWALD: While morning is shining,
  Your garlands entwine;

Ere evening closes,
Gather your posies,
Jasmine and roses,
    Sweet eglantine!
DORCAS: While yet it is daylight,
    Rejoice in the day;
        Nought to repent of,
        Breath be content of,
        Fragrant with scent of
    Newly mown hay!
BOTH: Night will come soon enough—
    Starlight nor moon enough!
    While there is noon enough,
        Let us be gay!
OSWALD: No grace is in grief, and
    No virtue in tears!
        Come what may after,
        Youth and its laughter
        Piercing the rafter,
    Gladden the spheres!
DORCAS: Tomorrow we'll sorrow
    But now let us sing!
        Happy to-day be,
        Joyous and gay be,
        Plucking while may be
    Blossoms of spring!
OSWALD: Each gift of creation
    Is heaven's envoy;
        Ne'er a bud springeth,
        Ne'er a bird singeth,
        But to earth bringeth
    Tidings of joy!
DORCAS: Oh! list to the message
    The hemispheres voice!
        "Folly is sadness,
        Misery, madness,
        Holy is gladness—
    Thine is the choice!"
BOTH: Night will come soon enough—

SYDNEY GRUNDY AND ARTHUR SULLIVAN

Starlight nor moon enough!
While there is noon enough,
Let us rejoice!

DOROTHY *is seen coming down the terrace.*

RECITATIVE.

DORCAS: My mistress comes. Thyself thy missive
　　give.

DOROTHY *advances towards her.*

OSWALD: Madam, I bow.

DOROTHY: Sir, who art thou?

OSWALD: Servant of one whose name I must not tell.
　　This from his hand—and from his heart as well.

DOROTHY *reads the letter.*

TRIO.—DOROTHY, DORCAS, and OSWALD.

DOROTHY: Oh, tell me, what is a maid to say?
　　What is a maid to do?
　When heart says "Go," and duty "Stay,"
　　And she'd to both be true?
　　Oh, tell me, what is a maid to say?
　　Shall it be rice or rue?
　When heart says "Yea," and duty "Nay,"
　　What is a maid to do?

TRIO: Yea or nay?
　　Go or stay?
　　To which be false, to which be true?
　When a maiden wavers 'twixt yea and nay—
　　Shall it be rice or rue?

OSWALD: Thou askest what is a maid to say,
　　What is a maid to do?
　I answer, if her heart say yea,
　　Her duty says so too.

DORCAS: I can but tell thee what I should say,
　　Tell thee what I should do;
　I'd go in showers of rice away,
　　And leave behind the rue.

TRIO: Yea or nay?
        Go or stay?
    To which be false, to which be true?
  When a maiden wavers 'twixt yea and nay—
        Shall it be rice or rue?
Exeunt DORCAS *and* OSWALD *severally.*

RECITATIVE and SONG.—DOROTHY.

Why weep and wait? Why hesitate?
Too soon is better than too late!
Ah, yes, I wait; but do not weep;
Thy love has rocked my tears to sleep.

Red of the rose-bud, white of the May,
Why are ye fragrant? Why are ye gay?
Why are ye blithe as blithe can be?
Whisper your secret low to me!
Why do ye droop when day is done?
Is it because ye love the sun?
Why do ye smile through tears of dew?
Is it because the sun loves you?
Red of the rose-bud, white of the May,
That is your secret, tell me not nay.
Sing the old song that for ever is new,
Ye love your love, and your love loves you.

Breast of the robin, why dost thou blush?
Whence is thy music, throat of the thrush?
Why do ye flit from tree to tree?
Warble your secret low to me!
Why do ye roam the sky above?
Is it in search of your true love?
Why do ye build yourselves a nest?
Is it because your love is blest?
Breast of the robin, why dost thou blush?
Where is thy music, throat of the thrush?
Fear not to whisper thy secret to me,
Thou lov'st thy love, and thy love loves thee.

Red of the rose-bud, white hawthorn bush,
Breast of the robin, song of the thrush,
I am as happy as happy as ye,
I love my love, and my love loves me!

Exit.

Enter JOHN MANNERS, *looking cautiously about him.*

MANNERS: Beshrew the knave! What hath become of him? Can they
have laid him by the heels? or may it be, love hath outpaced his
messenger? Ne'er have I ventured quite so close before. I greet thee,
Haddon! whose historic gates, open to all the world, close only
against me. And yet I love thee, Haddon, every tree and stone; for
thou art part of her and she is part of thee. I tread the grass her
feet have trod to-day; the blooms that smiled upon her, smile on
me; and in the scented breeze, I seem to feel her breath upon my
cheek!

SONG.—MANNERS.

The earth is fair
And a beauty rare
Bespangles lake and lea,
Ere day is done
And the setting sun
Dips down beneath the sea;
But never a sun in the skies afar
Bright as the eyes of my lady are,
My lady who loves me!
Where in the shining frame above,
Where in the great design,
Where in the world is found a love
Like unto mine and thine?
Like unto thine and mine, love!
Like unto mine and thine!

When pale afar
Is the evening star—
Sweet orphan of the night!—
Creation sleeps,
But its spirit keeps

Her virgin lamp alight;
Yet never a star in the heavens above
Pure as the soul of my lady love,
   Pure as the troth I plight!
Where in the shining frame on high,
   Where in the great design,
Where is the love in earth or sky
   Like unto thine and mine?
   Like unto mine and thine, love!
   Like unto thine and mine!

DOROTHY *appears on the terrace.*

DUET.—DOROTHY and MANNERS.

DOROTHY: Sweetly the morn doth break,
   When love is nigh;
Hues of the rainbow take
   Landscape and sky;
Gaily the sun doth shine
   Over my head;
High heaven itself is mine,
   Sorrow is dead.
Ever for thy dear sake
   Happy am I;
Sweetly the morn doth break,
   When love is nigh!
MANNERS: In my life's chalice, love,
   Thou art the wine!
DOROTHY: Now shines the sun above,
   Now art thou mine!
BOTH: Hues of the rainbow take
   Landscape and sky;
Sweetly the morn doth break,
   When love is nigh!
DOROTHY: Kneel not to me!
MANNERS: To whom else should I kneel?
   A loyal subject bends before his queen;
   And mine art thou!
DOROTHY: Hush! not so loud! Not long have I to stay.

Moments are precious.

MANNERS: When they are with thee.

DOROTHY: Nay, let me speak; for I have much to say.
    Our cousin Rupert comes to-day to wed me.

MANNERS: Let twenty cousins come, I fear them not!
    Thy word is pledged.

DOROTHY: And 'tis an easy task
    To keep an oath one hath no will to break.
    But what are vows, if they are vowed in vain?
    My father will not hearken to thy suit.

MANNERS: What says he?

DOROTHY: That thou must lay down thine arms,
    Ere he will hearken.

MANNERS: I, forswear the king?

DOROTHY: Oh, tell me, sweetheart, is thy love so great
    That thou wouldst do this for thy true love's sake?

MANNERS: Great is my love—greater than lord or
    king—
    But there is one thing greater than my love,
    One thing that e'en for thine I cannot do,
    And that thou askest me!

DOROTHY: Dost thou refuse?

MANNERS: False to myself, I should be false to thee,
    And heaven would curse our love; I should not dare
    To wear a garland so ignobly won,
    Lest with my touch I soiled it. It would drop,
    Withered and wan, in ashes, at my feet,
    Its perfumes changed to odours of decay.
    Nay, sweetheart mine, I will not make thy face—
    My noonday sun—my morning, evening star—
    A haunting spectre, symbol of my shame!

DOROTHY: That is thine answer?

MANNERS: There could be but one.

DOROTHY: Now am I thine for ever! Oh, my love,
    That is the answer I had prayed of thee!
    Hadst thou said aye, my love for thee had died.
    My word I would have kept: but in my heart
    Thine image would have fallen from its shrine.
    Thine in the flesh I might have been; but now,

Thine in the spirit I shall be for ever!

MANNERS: All angels guard thee!

DOROTHY: Hark! the tocsin bell!

Farewell, beloved!

MANNERS: Sweetheart, fare thee well!

Exeunt.

Enter PURITANS.

CHORUS OF PURITANS.

Down with princes, down with peoples!
Down with churches, down with steeples!
Down with love and down with marriage!
Down with all who keep a carriage!
Down with lord and down with lady—
Up with everything that's shady!

Down with life and down with laughter!
    Down with landlords, down with land!
Whom the soil belongs to after,
    We could never understand!
Pleasure—we can do without it;
    Down with Court and down with king;
And—just while we are about it—
    Down with every blessed thing!

Enter RUPERT VERNON.

RUPERT: My faithful friends, you have just been singing, with that accuracy of time and purity of tone which characterize all your vocal efforts, these admirable sentiments, amongst others, "Down with love, and down with marriage; down with landlords, down with land!" And truly these things are vanities—in the abstract; but in the concrete they possess a certain substance. In the abstract, I, Rupert Vernon, am a vanity.

PURITANS: Yea, verily.

RUPERT: But in the concrete, even I possess a certain substance.

PURITANS: Yea, verily.

RUPERT: These brief preliminary observations will have prepared you for the announcement that I am about to marry and become a landlord.

KILL-JOY: This be flat blasphemy!

RUPERT: I was once of that opinion myself. But ever since it hath become a question whether my title to this highly attractive residential property is not superior to that of my cousin, its present occupant, I have given much attention to the subject. As I may shortly be in a position to keep a carriage myself, I am not quite so persuaded as I was of the necessity of "downing" with everybody who indulges in that very harmless luxury.

NICODEMUS (*lifting his hands*): Odd's fish! odd's fish!

RUPERT: I fail to see anything odd's fish about it. Then again, our attitude with regard to the land question—is it quite sound? or is it all sound and no sense?

BARNABAS: There be one land and there be one people, and to the one people the one land belongeth.

RUPERT: Quite so, quite so, my good Barnabas. That is our way of putting it—in public. But this is not the hustings, and as private individuals we know perfectly well that there is more than one people—in fact, there are a great many people; and how is the one land to belong to all of them?

SIMEON: The state is the people. Let the land belong to the state.

RUPERT: Thou art minded that the occupier should pay his rent to the state.

PURITANS: No rent! no rent!

RUPERT: But if the occupier is to pay no rent, then each occupier becomes his own landlord.

PURITANS: Even so!

RUPERT: But in that case, you have more landlords than ever.

PURITANS: So we have! (*All scratch their heads*)

RUPERT: Nor is the subject of celibacy as simple as it appeared. Ever since it was arranged that the disputed title to the Haddon estates should be settled by my marriage with fair Mistress Dorothy, my views upon this matter also have undergone a change. I feel the need of female sympathy. Nobody sympathizes with us, and when one comes to think of it, why should they?

PURITANS: Why should they?

RUPERT: It must be admitted that we have made ourselves fairly obnoxious of late. We have been particularly busy, and our business has chiefly consisted in interfering with everybody else's. First and foremost, we have abolished the playhouse.

PURITANS: Grace be praised!

RUPERT: Secondly, we have forbidden dance music in all place of public resort.

KILL-JOY: We have robbed the devil of his best tunes.

RUPERT: But to give that ingenious gentleman his due, he has to some extent circumvented us; for, by the simple expedient of playing the Old Hundredth in double time, he has succeeded in evolving from that venerable air something suspiciously resembling the carnal and pernicious polka. (PURITANS *groan*) Thirdly, to the end that none shall profane the Sabbath by enjoying it, or shall imperil his soul by improving his mind, we have shut all museums, parks, and picture galleries, and turned the day of rest into a night of rust.

PURITANS: Grace be praised!

RUPERT: Fourthly, having deprived the populace of all means of innocent recreation, we have compelled them to seek solace in the consumption of strong drink.

NICODEMUS: Nay, verily; have we not closed all inns and taverns?

RUPERT: It is true that wholesome and necessary refreshment, either for man or beast, can no longer be procured in an open and honourable fashion; but I can give you my personal assurance that there exist scores of places where any quantity of deleterious concoctions can be obtained in a stealthy and disreputable manner.

PURITANS (*with unction*): Grace be praised!

BARNABAS: Verily, these be notable good works.

RUPERT: But who's the better for them, Barnabas? Who is the better for us? I will go a step further. Are we the better for ourselves?

PURITANS (*look at one another*): Ask us another!

RUPERT: I will ask you another. Are we comely to look upon?

PURITANS: Nay, verily!

RUPERT: Do we not consistently do everything we can to make everybody about us uncomfortable?

PURITANS: Yea, verily.

RUPERT: Do we enjoy ourselves?

KILL-JOY: All life is sack-cloth and ashes.

SIMEON: But our reward is to come.

RUPERT: Are ye sure of that? I have no wish to pose as an alarmist, but suppose we are making a bad debt? After a life spent in the mortification of the flesh, it would be a crowning mortification if it turned out that the flesh was not meant to be mortified; and it would be peculiarly irritating to discover that the flesh was intended to enjoy itself at the precise moment when he had no longer any flesh to enjoy.

BARNABAS: Marry come up!

RUPERT: Well, Barnabas, continue. Let us suppose, for the sake of argument, that "marry" did "come up"—what then?

BARNABAS: I have nought more to say.

RUPERT: Then hold thy peace, and hearken to a wiser tongue than thine.

SONG.—RUPERT.

I've heard it said,
And it may be read
In many a trusty tome,
How, when augurs met
On the parapet
Of the walls of ancient Rome,
As the two passed by,
Each winked an eye
With a candour confidential,
Or stroked his nose—
Which, goodness knows—
But it isn't at all essential.
For every man,
Since the world began,
Had his idiosyncrasee,
And to lunch off a moan
And dine on a groan
With a trickling tear for tea—
Well, it may suit you
From your point of view,
But it doesn't at all suit me!
As I don't rejoice
In a deep bass voice—
Well, it doesn't at all suit me.

Though the world be bad,
It's the best to be had;
And therefore, Q.E.D.,
Though it mayn't suit you
And a chosen few,
It's a good enough world for me.

Examples show
That we needn't go
So far as to ancient Rome,
For it just occurs
Unto me, good sirs,
There are humbugs nearer home.
When you style the spheres
A vale of tears,
Don't you rather beg the question?
Remember, bards,
It's on the cards,
It is nothing but indigestion.
For every man,
Since the world began,
Had his little infirmitee,
And is apt to mistake
What is only an ache
For profound philosophee.
He is not the sphinx
He sublimely thinks,
But a man very much like me!
Not a demon fell,
Or an archangel,
But a man very much like me.
Though the world be bad,
It's the best to be had;
And therefore Q.E.D.,
Though it mayn't suit you
And a chosen few,
It's a good enough world for me.

Exeunt.
Re-enter DORCAS *and* CHORUS.

SYDNEY GRUNDY AND ARTHUR SULLIVAN

Finale of Act I.

Chorus.

The bonny bridegroom cometh
    To meet the bonny bride,
  Let all the gates of Haddon
    Their portals open wide!

Rupert and the Puritans *re-appear on the terrace.*

The bonny bridegroom cometh—
    Your breath together draw!
  Prepare to bid him welcome
    With a hip, hip, hip—oh law!

All avert their faces at the sight of the Puritans.

Rupert: Our first appearance is not a success.

Simeon: Well, not a triumph.

Nicodemus: A succes d'estime.

Barnabas: Or less.

Rupert: Ladies fair, I pray you,
    Do not be afraid;
  Let us not dismay you,
    We but ply our trade.

Puritans: Do not so disdain us,
  We but ply our trade!

Chorus: Though the objects pain us,
  They but ply their trade.

Rupert: Once we close the portals,
    Once we shut the shop,
  We're like other mortals,
    Out upon the hop!

Puritans: Out upon the hop!

Chorus: Once they close the portals,
    Once they shut the shop,
  They're like other mortals,
    Out upon the hop!

Rupert: I pray you, pretty ladies,
    Before this audience ends,
  To let me do the honours
    And introduce my friends.

Sing-Song Simeon

DORCAS (*shaking head*): Not an Endymion!

RUPERT: Nicodemus Knock-knee.

NANCE: Sanctimonious cockney!

RUPERT: Barnabas Bellows-to-Mend.

DORCAS: All of them fellow to mend!

RUPERT: Kill-Joy Candlemas.

CHORUS: Enough! enough! we have suffered galore,
      We cannot suffer more!
        Oh, let's see the back of you,
        Every man-jack of you,
    All of you sillies and all of you sights!
        The sight of old fogies
        That blow up like bogies,
  And keep one awake in the dead of the nights.
        Get away! get away! get away!

They go up in a dudgeon.

RUPERT (*to Audience*): Between ourselves, I candidly confess,
    That I expected neither more nor less.
    (*to* PURITANS). My faithful friends, I do not mind confessing
    To all of you, whom I am now addressing,
    That, as a lot, you are not prepossessing.
        It's no use blinking it!

PURITANS: We were just thinking it!

RUPERT: Ladies, pretty ladies, second thoughts are best;
    Pregnant is the proverb, time's the only test.
        Come, ladies fair
        Beyond compare,
      And list to my confessions;
        Be warned by me,
        And never be
      Deceived by first impressions.

ENSEMBLE.

MEN.	WOMEN.
Go, ladies fair,	Come, ladies fair,
Beyond compare—	Beyond compare—
And list to his confessions.	And list to his confessions.

When I was but a little lad,
And cake and toffee made me glad,
   And high the sun at noon!
My mother came to me one day,
When I was in the field at play,
   With jam upon a spoon.
It looked so nice, I thought not twice,
The jam had vanished in a trice—
   Quite frank are these confessions!
Alas, the jam concealed a pill
Which made me very, very ill—
   Deceived by first impressions!
Chorus: Oh, joy! the jam concealed a pill
   Which made him very, very ill—
   Deceived by first impressions!

   Quoth Dr. Syntax, one fine day,
  "Rupert, I have a word to say."
     (I had just told a cram)
So tenderly he took my hand,
His tone was so polite and bland,
   I followed like a lamb.
But once upstairs his manner freezed,
And all at once he seemed displeased,
   As with Aeneas, Dido!
Then, quick as thought he seized a birch
And fairly knocked me off my perch—
   Whack, whack, whack-fol-de-riddle-i-do!
Chorus: Whack-fol-de-riddle-i-do!
Rupert: Now, ladies fair,
   Beyond compare
Be warned by my confessions;
All: You surely see
   The vanity—
Of trusting first impressions.
   Whack, whack, whack-fol-de-riddle-I-do!
Re-enter Sir George, Lady Vernon, *and* Dorothy.

SIR G.: Hail, Cousin Rupert, welcome to our heart!
  Though scarce we know thee in this habit homely.
RUPERT: It doth not suit me, but before we part
  I hope to change it for a grab more comely.
LADY V.: A bridegroom's?
RUPERT: Aye, if this sweet maiden wills.
SIR G.: This maiden aye her father's wish fulfils.
RUPERT: Cousin fair, to thee I offer
  Soul and body, heart and hand.
SIR G.: In exchange to thee we proffer
  Beauty, duty, house, and land.
LADY V.: Husband, hear me! husband, listen!
    Let our daughter's heart reply.
  In her eyes the teardrops glisten.
    If she wed him, she will die!
DOROTHY: Father, hear me; father, listen!
  If I wed him, I shall die!

ENSEMBLE.

DOROTHY: Father, hear me, father, hear me;
  If I wed him I shall die!
DORCAS: Only hear her, only listen!
  If she wed him, she will die!
LADY V.: Husband, hear her, husband, hear her
  If she wed him, she will die!
RUPERT: Cousin fair, to thee I offer
  Soul and body, heart and hand.
SIR G. AND CHORUS: If she wed him, she will die!

SOLO.—DOROTHY.

When, yestereve, I knelt to pray,
    As thou hast taught me to,
I seemed to hear the angels say,
    "To thine own heart be true."
Heaven breathed a message through the sphere!
    Heaven breathes it every day,
To all who have the ears to hear,

The wisdom to obey.
By golden day and silver night
It rings all nature through;
For ever, in the angels' sight,
To thine own heart be true.
Though storms uprise
And cloud the skies,
And thorns where roses grew;
Come sun or snow,
Come weal or woe.
To thine own heart be true.

CHORUS: Though storms uprise, etc.

DOROTHY (*kneels*): Father, forgive!

SIR G.: Rise! to thy chamber, thou rebellious maid!
My will is law, and law must be obeyed.

DOROTHY: Father, forgive!

SIR G.: I ask not words of duty, I ask for deeds.
Away, away!

LADY V.: She doth but stay
Farewell to say!

DORCAS: Sweet mistress, all my heart is thine!

SIR G.: No longer art thou daughter mine!

RUPERT: We are refused!

PURITANS: We are! we are!

CHORUS: Hurray, hurray,
Oh, blessed day!

RUPERT and PURITANS: A plague upon our natal star
We are refused! We are! we are!

ENSEMBLE.

SIR G.: Away! away!
My word obey!

DOROTHY: Sir, I obey!

LADY V. and DORCAS: Oh, fateful day!

RUPERT: Dismay! Dismay!

PURITANS: Oh, fateful day!

CHORUS: Away! away!
His word obey!

SIR G., RUPERT, PURITANS.	DOROTHY.	THE REST.

Thy duty, with
    unerring hand,
Dictates the
    rightful way!
It is a father's
    to command!
Dare not to disobey!
	Thy duty, with
	    unerring hand,
	Dictates the
	    rightful way!
	
	I dare not disobey!
		Thy duty, with
		    unerring hand,
		Dictates the
		    rightful way!
		It is for conscience
		    to command!
		Dare not to disobey!

END OF Act I

Act II

SCENE 1.—DOROTHY VERNON'S *Door.*
RUPERT *and the* PURITANS *are discovered, sheltering from the storm.*

CHORUS.

PURITANS: Hoarsely the wind is howling—
  Bitterly bites the blast—
 The midnight cat is prowling—
  The rain is falling fast—
   But what of that?
 We'll back ourselves against the howling wind
 And the nocturnal cat—
  At two to one, bar none.
RUPERT: And not a layer find
 Even at that.
PURITANS: Even at that.
RUPERT: The wind falls fast,
   In icy blasts:
 It's the sort of day when people say
  It's much too bad to last.
PURITANS: But it lasts!
RUPERT: It lasts!
PURITANS: It lasts!
RUPERT: My good friend, Simeon, thou who singest songs and art
 by way of being a musician, tell me, what is thy private judgment
 on these strains with which it is our habit to beguile our lighter
 moments?
SIMEON: I'sooth, they be saintly airs.
RUPERT: At the same time, dost thou not think, something a trifle
 more melodious—
KILL-JOY: Melody! 'tis the invention of Satan!
BARNABAS: To us hath been revealed the higher law, that discord is the
 soul of all true harmony.
RUPERT: Barnabas, thou wert born before thy time. Two centuries
 hence, and thou wouldst be a leader amongst musicians; but as
 things are, thou art an anachronism.

KILL-JOY: Verily, we are all anachronisms.

SIMEON: But conscience is a great comforter.

NICODEMUS Even in such weather as this.

BARNABAS: Troth, 'tis a gruesome night!

RUPERT (*glancing at window*): But they seem to be enjoying themselves within. High jinks, within. And why are we out of it? This feast is given in our especial honour, and here we are cooling our heels in this particularly moist and most unpleasant atmosphere, simply because our conscientious scruples will not permit us to countenance such carnal junkettings. But for our consciences we should probably at this moment be enjoying a stoup of something hot—

KILL-JOY: With spice in it! (ALL *sigh and gaze at the windows*)

RUPERT: Our withdrawal has not cast that gloom over the proceedings which might have been anticipated.

SIMEON: But heed them not! We are the salt of the earth.

RUPERT: My faithful Simeon, is not that an additional reason why we should be kept in a dry place? This excess of moisture without and this phenomenal aridity within are beginning to tell upon me. I feel my Puritanic principles are tottering. It will do me a world of good to refresh myself at the uncompromising fount of The McCrankie.

NICODEMUS: But where is he?

RUPERT: He is certainly late, but he has a long way to come. The Island of Rum is situate in a remote part of the west coast of Scotland; but between you and me, I sometimes wish it were further. The McCrankie is a Puritan above proof, and a little of him goes a long way—especially when he accompanies himself on the national instrument. (PURITANS *groan*) Let us hope he will leave it behind him. (*The bagpipes are heard in the distance*) Oh, this is worse than the weather!

Enter THE MCCRANKIE.

SONG.—MCCRANKIE.

My name it is McCrankie,
I am lean an' lang an' lanky,
I'm a Moody an' a Sankey,
    Wound upo' a Scottish reel!

Pedantic an' puncteelious,
Severe an' superceelious,
Preceese an' atra-beelious—
    But meanin' vera weel.
I don't objec tae whiskey,
But I say a' songs are risky,
An' I think a' dances frisky
    An' I've pit the fuitlichts oot!
I am the maist dogmatical,
Three-cornered, autocratical,
Funereal, fanatical,
    O' a' the cranks aboot!

I'd pit a stap tae jokin',
An' I wadna sanction smokin';
An' my nose I wad be pokin'
    Into ilka body's way.
I'd use my power censorial
In manner dictatorial;
To naebody's memorial
    Attention wad I pay;
I'd stap the kittens' playin'
An' forbid the horses' neighin',
But oh, not the ass's brayin',
    For I love the ass's bray!
I am the maist mechanical,
Ofeecious, puritanical,
Pragmatic an' tyrannical
    Production o' the day!

RUPERT: So here thou art at last! Thou hast been long on the way.

McCRAN: Houts, mon, business maun be attended tae.

RUPERT: Business? What business?

McCRAN: If thou but ken't how mony gude folk I had made meeserable, thou'd say I'd nae wasted my time. I'd scarce set foot upo' t' bo't that was to hae brought me frae t'Eel o' Rum, when I behelt a sicht that froze me vera blud. A sailor-laddie, gangin' on a cruise, a cuittlin' an' a cuddlin' a braw lassie on t' quay itsel'!

RUPERT: Perhaps she was his sister?

McCran: Aiblins, aiblins! I care nae boddle! Was I tae staun by an see cuittlin' an' cuddlin' i' a public place? Na, na. Sae I jist steppit ashore an' charged 'em wi' disorderly behaviour. That's hoo I missed t' bo't.

Rupert: Any more adventures?

McCran: The neist sicht that I seen was some wee bairns singin' an' dancin' i' t' oopen air. I jist gang'd up tae 'em, and somethin' i' ma vera face took the de'il oot' 'em. I said, "Hae ye a singin' an' a dancin' leecence?" They said they hadna; sae I took 'em tae t' jile, an' when I left 'em greetin' oot their een, I couldna help fa'in on ma knees, an' giein' the Laird thanks for ha'en made a mon sae unco guid as me.

Rupert: No doubt, McCrankie, no doubt, as a work of art thou dost Providence infinite credit.

McCran: An' ye may say that. T'best day's work it aye did. I aye said that.

Rupert: But there is one little matter which rather perplexes me, if I may mention it without offence.

McCran: Oot wi' it!

Rupert: I have never been able to reconcile thy notorious objection to the costume of the corps de ballet with this exceedingly liberal display of thine own personal attractions.

McCran: Mon, it is saved from offence by the deegnity o' the kilt.

Rupert: Which is its dignity? That tobacco pouch there?

McCran: Tat, mon, be ma sporran.

Rupert: Or that arrangement in petticoats?

McCran: Tat, mon, be ma philabeg. Houts, thou doil'd dotard, thou may lauch thy fill, but Scots wha hae nae breeks aye worn, nae breeks sall they aye wear.

Rupert: What art thou about now?

McCran: Aweel, aweel, I was jist baskin' i' t' licht o' my ain coontenance, an' gie'in' thanks that I was made sae muckle mair guid that ithers.

Rupert: But, McCrankie, my old comrade, strictly between ourselves, dost think that this exuberant virtue of ours is altogether a matter for thanksgiving? It makes life somewhat dull, doth it not?

McCran (*producing flask*): Aweel, aweel, life hae its campensation. Here's t' ye! (*drinks*) Hae a drappie? (Puritans *gather round*)

RUPERT: I don't mind if I do. (*Drinks and returns flask.* PURITANS *cough*)

McCRAN (*puts flask back in his sporran*): Hae ye caulds, a' o' ye?

RUPERT: My friends, you may withdraw. The McCrankie and I are about to propound the Puritan programme of posterity, and it is desirable that he should not be interrupted. Withdraw gracefully, if ye can—but withdraw.

SIMEON: As usual.

NICODEMUS: Out of it.

PURITANS: Always out of it!

Exeunt PURITANS.

McCRAN: Hae they ga'en awa'?

RUPERT: They have not withdrawn gracefully, but they have withdrawn.

DUET.—RUPERT and McCRANKIE.

RUPERT: There's no one by—no prying eye—

McCRANKIE: Our solemn secret tae espy—

BOTH: So let us plainly say—

RUPERT: Could we create the world anew,—

McCRANKIE: What we wad vera quickly do,—

BOTH: If we but had our way!

RUPERT: Like Joshua, we would stop the sun—

McCRANKIE: The thing is vera simply done—

BOTH: If we but had our way!

RUPERT: We'd pit an end ta heat an' licht—

McCRANKIE: An' bring aboot eternal nicht—

BOTH: If we but had our way!

RUPERT: We'd supervise the plants and flowers—

McCRANKIE: Prescribe 'em early closin' hours—

BOTH: If we but had our way!

RUPERT: We would forbid the rose to smell—

McCRANKIE: We'd re-instate the curfew bell—

BOTH: If we but had our way!

RUPERT: No man, in influenza's throes,

McCRANKIE: Suld be allo'ed ta blaw his nose—

BOTH: If we but had our way!

RUPERT: No cock should crow, no bird should sing,—

McCrankie: Naebody suld dae onything—

Rupert: Without our license, sealed and signed:—

McCrankie: For we wad dominate monkind—

Both: If we but had our way!

Rupert: We were not, through some freak of earth, Consulted at the planet's birth—

Both: Though we'd a lot to say!

McCrankie: Had we been on creation's scene,
A great improvement there'd ha' been—

Both: If we but had our way.

Rupert: But somehow we were clean forgot,

McCrankie: That's why we'll make things piping hot—

Both: And ye the piper pay.

McCrankie: We'll tax ye oop an' tax ye doon,

Rupert: We'll tax the country, tax the toon,—

Both: If we but had our way.

Rupert: We'll tax ye hip, an' tax ye thigh,—

McCrankie: An' sen' the rate-book oop lift-high,—

Both: And cry, hurray, hurray!

Rupert: An' what becomes o' science, art,

McCrankie: The law, the temple, an' the mart,

Both: We naether ken nor care!

Rupert: We only know, as sure as shot—

McCrankie: Wha pays his scot an' bears his lot—

Both: A lot will have to bear.

Rupert: We only know, our lack of sense

McCrankie: Is inconceivably immense!

Rupert: And now, we hope, ye plainly see

McCrankie: That ye are bigger fools than we—

Both: If we but have our way!

The door is cautiously opened, and Dorcas *appears.* Rupert *and* The McCrankie *withdraw into the shadow.* Dorcas *comes down the steps.*

Dorcas: Not a sound! Not a whisper! Where can Oswald be? This is the hour, and this the trysting place.

Rupert *and* The McCrankie *advance—she screams.*

McCran: Dinna be frichtened, leddy.

Dorcas: Who art thou?

SYDNEY GRUNDY AND ARTHUR SULLIVAN

RUPERT: Permit me to introduce my old friend, The McCrankie, from the
Island of Rum—a Scotch puritan of the most uncompromising type.
McCRAN: An' wha is this braw lassie?
RUPERT: Mistress Dorcas, handmaiden to fair Mistress Dorothy.
McCRAN: I am richt glad tae mak thine acquaintance.
DORCAS: So am not I. Hands off!
McCRAN: Hout awa', leddy. The nicht is dark—
RUPERT: And there is no one looking.
DORCAS: So much the worse!
McCRAN: Sae muckle the better! Thou'rt a sonsie lassie.
DORCAS: Fie on ye! Fie! Ye are a brace of ill-mannered knaves, and
ought both to be clapped in the stocks!

TRIO.—DORCAS, RUPERT, and McCRANKIE.

RUPERT: Hoity-toity, what's a kiss?
McCRANKIE: 'Tis nae vera shockin'!
RUPERT: Do not take the thing amiss!
McCRANKIE: Lass, there's nae ane leukin'!
DORCAS: Hoity-toity, what's a kiss?
    Kissing goes by favour!
RUPERT: And when the kiss
    Is a stolen bliss—
McCRANKIE: The sweeter is the savour!
DORCAS: Upon my word,
        I never heard
    A statement more surprising!
        Aren't ye afraid
        Of with a maid
    Your conscience compromising?
TRIO: Upon the light
        And starry night,
    We might consult the latter;
        But when the maid
        Is in the shade,
    It's quite another matter.
RUPERT: Hoity-toity, who's afraid?
McCRANKIE: When there's nae ane leukin'!
RUPERT: I could ne'er resist a maid—

McCRANKIE: When she shows her stockin'!
DORCAS: Hoity-toity, man, be mum!
  Hast thou had a glassie?
RUPERT: My friend hath come
  From the Isle of Rum—
McCRANKIE: An' thou'rt a braw, wee lassie!
DORCAS: Behave thyself,
    Thou Highland elf,
  Thy conduct is past bearing;
    I thought ye both
    Had taken oath,
  Frivolity foreswearing.
TRIO: Like every man,
    A Puritan
  Admires a waist that's taper,
    And on the sly
    Will wink his eye
  And cut his little caper!
RUPERT: Hoity-toity, what's an oath?
McCRANKIE: Eyes were made for hookin'.
RUPERT: We are very human, both—
McCRANKIE: When there's nae ane leukin'!
DORCAS: Hoity-toity, things have come
  To a pretty passie!
RUPERT: The Isle of Rum
  Is a trifle glum—
McCRANKIE: An' thou'rt a bonny lassie!
DORCAS: Thou horrid thing!
    Thou Highland fling!
  I'm sure thou'st had a glassie!
    I won't by you—(*box*)
    Or any two—(*box*)
  Be called a bonny lassie!

ENSEMBLE.

RUPERT and McCRANKIE.	DORCAS.
Oh, hist and whist!	Oh, hist and whist,
Now, don't resist!	Now, do desist,

Why make so great a clatter?	Or I'll create a clatter!
There's none to see,	Do set me free,
So what the d—,	And let me be,
The De'il doth it matter?	And cease your silly chatter.

Thunder. Exeunt Rupert *and* McCrankie.

Finale of Act II.

Quartet.

Dorcas: The West wind howls,
    The thunder rolls,
  But love keeps warm my heart!
    Oh, mistress dear,
    To-night and here,
  Sweet mistress, must we part?

Enter Oswald.

Oswald: The horses are saddled and dark is the night,
  The stars in the firmament favour our flight;
  Each planet its splendour hath graciously veiled;
  And the chaste moon herself her effulgence hath paled.

Dorcas: But the planets are there,
  Though their glory they hide;
  Though a mask they may wear,
    They will smile on the bride!
  The stars keep their vigil above her;
  Oh, Oswald, dear Oswald, I love her.

Oswald: Ah, happy maid,
    A wife so soon to be,
  To be beloved
    By one so fair as thee!

Dorcas: Not now! not now!
    To love's sweet vow
  I'll listen all life long;
    Sing love to me,
    And thine I'll be
  And live upon thy song;
    But sing not now!
  If they should take her!

If they should pursue!
Do not forsake her,
   Oh, my lover true!
Promise me, Oswald, promise thy bride,
      That if thou leavst me a maid forlorn,
      To weep the day that I e'er was born,
Thou wilt not leave her side!
OSWALD: I swear!
DORCAS: Now art thou mine,
   For ever mine!
OSWALD: And I for ever thine!
   Thunder.
MANNERS (*off*): Flash, lightning, flash,
      And roll, thou thunder, roll!
The heaven crash,
   But peace is in my soul;
For love is there,
   Serene and blest,
And everywhere
   Where love is, there is rest.
Enter MANNERS.
TRIO: Flash, lightning, flash,
      And roll, thou thunder, roll!
Thou canst not crush!
   Love reigns from pole to pole!
MANNERS: And through the black
      Abyss above
   Love rolls thee back,
      For thou thyself art love.
DORCAS AND OSWALD: For love is there,
      And everywhere
   Where love is, there is rest.
TRIO: Flash, lightning, flash,
      And roll, thou thunder, roll!
   Where love is, there is rest.
The door opens and DOROTHY *appears.* DORCAS *goes up to close the door.*
Exit OSWALD.
MANNERS: Oh, heart's desire
      I see thee once again!

I seem to hear the heavenly choir
　　Sing, life is not in vain.
When thou art nigh, oh, true my love,
　　Again the sky is blue,
　　　There is no darkness now!
DOROTHY: There is no light,
　　When thou art far away;
Thine absence is to me the night,
　　Thy presence is the day;
For when I am with thee, my love
　　Another world I see,
　　　There is no darkness now!
BOTH: There is no darkness, oh, my love!
Re-enter OSWALD.
OSWALD: The horses are waiting—
DORCAS: And ready am I!
MANNERS: The storm is abating—
　　Come, love, let us fly!
DOROTHY: Oh, grant me one moment!
OSWALD: The horses are waiting—
DOROTHY: Dear Haddon, good-bye!
MANNERS: Come, love, let us fly!
DOROTHY: Home of my girlhood, so happy, farewell!
　　I ne'er may look on thee
　　　Again—
　　Who can tell?
　　The stars shine upon thee!
　　　Farewell!
　Father, oh father, I love thee! Good-bye!
　　I have tried to obey thee—
　　　In vain!
　　　Sad am I!
　　Oh, love me, I pray thee!
　　　Good-bye!
A crash of thunder. She falls in MANNERS' *arms.*
DOROTHY: Why do the heavens roar? Is this thing sin
　　That I am doing for thy sake?
　Ghostly the night!
MANNERS: But calm aye follows storm!

DORCAS: Hush! what was that?
OSWALD: Thy heart thine ear deceives.
MANNERS: 'Twas nought!
DORCAS: Again! Again!
DOROTHY: See yonder form!
ALL: Hush! (*Pause*)
    'Twas but the twinkle of the rustling leaves.
MANNERS: Be not afraid! on my strong arm depend!
DORCAS: See! there is something!
OSWALD: Where?
MANNERS: Amongst the trees.
DORCAS: Yes, there is something moving!
DOROTHY: Saints defend! (*Pause*)
ALL: 'Twas but the branches swaying in the breeze
MANNERS: Now step lightly,
      Hold me tightly,
   Creep along by yonder wall.
ALL: Hush, step lightly!
      Hold me tightly!
  Where the deepest shadows fall.
      Heaven, befriend us!
      Saints defend us!
  Fare thee well, old Haddon Hall!
DOROTHY: Fare thee well,
  Home of my girlhood, so happy, farewell!
ALL: Now step lightly,
      Hold me tightly,
  Lightly let our footsteps fall.
  Exeunt, pursued by the PURITANS.

STORM.

As the storm dies away, the scene changes to THE LONG GALLERY, *where* SIR
GEORGE, LADY VERNON, *and* CHORUS *are discovered.*
Enter MAJOR DOMO.
MAJOR DOMO: Silence all! Attend your host!
   Silence all, and pledge the toast!
SIR G.: 'Tis an honoured old tradition
      Open house is Haddon Hall;

       SYDNEY GRUNDY AND ARTHUR SULLIVAN

Welcome all who seek admission,
  Gentle, simple, great and small.
Health and wealth to comrades present,
  Welcome one and all the same!
CHORUS: Health to peer and health to peasant!
  Health to squire and health to dame!

SONG.—SIR GEORGE.

  In days of old,
  When hearts were bold,
And the prize of the brave the fair,
  We danced and sang
  Till the rafters rang
And laughter was everywhere!
Our lives were lives of stress and storm,
But through our veins the blood ran warm—
  We only laughed the more!
  For mirth was mirth,
  And worth was worth
In the grand old days of yore!
CHORUS: To the grand old days of yore!
(*the following verse appears in the libretto but not in the vocal score*)
  In time gone by,
  A man would die
For his king and his country's sake;
  Then eyes of blue
  Spoke a Saxon true,
Who feared neither sword nor stake;
Then laughing love made glad the earth,
And men were not ashamed of mirth,
  And loud the table's roar;
  For breath was breath,
  And death was death
In the grand old days of yore.
CHORUS: To the grand old days of yore!

  Ere life is old
  And hearts grow cold,

And the autumn gathers grey,
    With soul and voice
    In your youth rejoice,
And merrily keep your May;
  Again let love and manly mirth
  And woman's beauty rule the earth
    As beauty ruled before;
     And once again
     Let men be men
    As they were in days of yore.

CHORUS: To the grand old days of yore!

Enter RUPERT *and* MCCRANKIE *bearing in* DORCAS, *followed by the* PURITANS.

RUPERT: Eloped, eloped! Betrayed, betrayed!
  Abetted by this tricksy maid!

MCCRANKIE: Ech, mon! ech mon! t' dochter's flown!

SIR G.: Is this my house, sir, or thine own?

RUPERT: Forgive my friend—let me express
  My sorrow for his zeal's excess;
    He has only just come
    From the Isle of Rum,
  And this is his native evening dress.

SIR G.: But why has he come—

LADY V. and DORCAS: Yes, why has he come—

CHORUS: Yes, why had he come from the Isle of Rum?

SIR G.: And having come—

LADY V. and DORCAS: Yes, having come—

CHORUS: Yes, having come from the Isle of Rum—

SIR G.: Cannot thy Gaelic friend be dumb?

ALL: Although he has come From the Isle of Rum.

MCCRANKIE: Eh, mon, eh, mon, ye dinna ken,
  T' dochter's gane wi' evil men!

SIR G.: What is this tale?

LADY V.: I fear me!

RUPERT: This tale I will succinctly tell,
  If you will only hear me.

CHORUS: Oh! tell the tale to us as well;
  A tearful tale, I fear me!

RUPERT: We were sheltering all
    Underneath a wall,

Very damp and most unhappy;
>   And to keep us warm
>   In the pelting storm—

McCRANKIE: We were hae'ing a wee drappie!

PURITANS: They were having a wee drappie!

RUPERT: We said so, friends!

McCRANKIE: We said, we a'
>   Were bidin' underneath a wa'—

RUPERT: Very damp—

McCRANKIE: An' maist unhappy!

PURITANS: Oh yes, we were damp,
>   And we all had a cramp,
>   But we had no wee drappie!

DORCAS and CHORUS: That's why you were unhappy?

PURITANS: That's why we were unhappy.

McCRANKIE: I was bidin' there
>   Wi' nae breeks tae wear—
>   An' a kilt's a wee bit draughty!

RUPERT: When one of the boys
>   He heard a noise—

McCRANKIE: An' we listened cool an' crafty.

SIMEON (*holding up his hand*): Please, I was the boy—
>   Who heard the noi—

CHORUS (*much interested*): And you listened cool and crafty.

RUPERT: To voices speaking—

McCRANKIE: Footsteeps creaking—

BOTH: Then a silence deep and dead.

PURITANS: Need we mention
>   Our attention
>   Was bestowed on what they said?

CHORUS: And what did the voices say?
>   Tell us, we pray!

RUPERT: Hush, step lightly!

McCRANKIE: Haud me tightly!

PURITANS: Lightly let your footsteps fall—
>   Lightly, lightly, lightly fall!

RUPERT: Forward I rushed, this saucy vixen grasping!

McCRANKIE: Forrit I fell, an' crackt a Scottish croon!

PURITANS: Backward we flew, until we pulled up gasping'!

McCrankie: I rose agen, but some ane knockt me doon!
Rupert: A sound of hoofs against the gravel ringing—
McCrankie: The cluds disperse, that had obscured the moon—
Rupert: We see a maiden to a horseman clinging!
McCrankie: We were too late—
Puritans: Or else we were too soon.
Rupert, McCrankie, Women: Too late! too late! too late!
Men: Or else we were too soon.
Sir G.: What means this tale? Why interrupt our sport,
  This intrigue of the kitchen to report?
Dorcas: It means that to-morrow
    Thy daughter and pride
  Will be, to thy sorrow,
    Her true lover's bride.
Sir G.: My daughter!
Lady V.: My daughter!
All: Thy daughter!
Rupert: My cousin and bride!
Dorcas: Away to the water
  They gallantly ride! (*Thunder*)
Sir G.: To horse—to horse—the fugitives pursue!
Chorus: To horse—to horse—the fugitives pursue!
Rupert, McCrankie, Puritans: To horse—to horse—but after you!
Sir G.: Fleet though the lightning's flash
    Vanish from view,
  Surely the thunder's crash
    Follows anew.
  I will, whatever hap,
    Press through the holt,
  Swift as the thunder-clap
    After the bolt!
Chorus: Fleet though the lightning's flash, etc.
Chorus: To horse! To horse!
Sir G.: Spare neither steed nor spur!
Chorus: To horse! To horse!
Rupert, McCrankie, Puritans: We will bring up the rear!
All: To horse! To horse! The fugitives pursue!
  Exeunt Sir George and a few of the Chorus, the rest gather
    round Lady Vernon.

LADY V.: In vain they will blunder
　　　Through halt and through brake;
　　Never yet did the thunder
　　　The lightening o'ertake!
　　NANCE, GERTRUDE,
DEBORAH: Farewell, our gracious hostess,
　　　Of children both bereft;
　　But love, obedience, troops of friends
　　　Unto thee still are left.
　　Not ours to break grief's sacred seal
　　　And on thy woe to dwell,
　　But ours to bend a humble knee
　　　And bid thee fond farewell.
　　Farewell! Farewell!
FULL CHORUS:
　　Time, the Avenger,
　　　Time, the Controller,
　　　　Time, that unravels the tangle of life,
　　Guard thee from danger,
　　　Prove thy consoler,
　　　　And make thee again happy mother and wife!
Exeunt LADY VERNON and DORCAS.
SERVANTS *enter, and extinguish the lights, one by one. The* CHORUS *disperse,
and gradually exeunt, singing:—*
　　Brief is all life;
　　Its storm and strife
　　　Time stills;
　　And through this dream
　　The nameless scheme
　　　Fulfils
　　Until one day
　　　Through space is hurled
　　　A vacant world,
　　Silent and grey.
*As the lamps are extinguished, the cold light of dawn steals through the
windows. The* SERVANTS *exeunt, and the curtain falls.*

END OF ACT II

Act III

Scene:—*The Ante-chamber.*
Enter Rupert *and* Chorus, *now arrayed in Puritan costume.*

Chorus.

(*Aloud*) Our heads we bow, the rod we kiss—
(*Aside*) Did ever you hear such a chorus as this?
  It's a Puritan notion of heavenly bliss!
(*Aloud*) The scales has fallen from our eyes—
(*Aside*) We're painfully conscious we're so many guys,
  And we're all of us telling a parcel of lies!
(*Aloud*) The truth at last we plainly see—
(*Aside*) Oh, hi diddle, diddle! between you and me,
  Our apparent conversion is fiddle-de-dee!
(*Aloud*) Oh, priceless gift! Oh blessed boon!
(*Aloud*) It must have been this identical tune
  The apocryphal quadruped perished so soon.

Ensemble.

Puritans (*Aloud*)	Chorus (*Aside*)
Our heads we bow, the rod we kiss—	Did ever you hear such a chorus as this?
	It's a Puritan notion of heavenly bliss!
The scales has fallen from our eyes—	We're painfully conscious we're so many guys,
	And we're all of us telling a parcel of lies!
The truth at last we plainly see—	Oh, hi diddle, diddle! between you and me,
	Our apparent conversion is fiddle-de-dee!
Oh, priceless gift! Oh blessed boon!	It must have been this identical tune
	The apocryphal quadruped perished so soon.

Chorus (*Aloud*): Oh blessed boon!

SYDNEY GRUNDY AND ARTHUR SULLIVAN

(*Aside*) Oh what a tune!

RUPERT: Very good—excellent! That will conclude our lesson for to-
day. As a reward for your good conduct I will now communicate
to you a piece of information which I feel sure you will receive
with feelings of the liveliest satisfaction. The law-suit, which,
since the somewhat abrupt departure of Mistress Dorothy with
a handsomer—ahem!—with another gentleman—I have been
prosecuting with the utmost vigour, has at last been terminated
in my favour. This hall and these estates now vest in me. Though
with my usual good taste I have not insisted on the immediate
evacuation of my cousin, Sir George, and his good lady, from
this day forth I am the Lord of Haddon—I alone. (CHORUS
continue reading, taking no notice of him. RUPERT *comes down*) My
announcement has not been received with the cordiality which I
had a right to expect. I have always understood that on such an
occasion it was customary for retainers, servants, peasants, etc., to
break out in a chorus expressive of delight and admiration.
(*Glances at* CHORUS) I have evidently been misinformed.

Enter LADY VERNON, *attended by* DORCAS.

RUPERT: 'Tis my fair cousin!

LADY V.: Sir, without waste of words, it is not our purpose to intrude
longer on thy hospitality. My husband awaits thee in the Eagle
Tower, prepared to yield to thee the muniments of Haddon and to
say farewell.

RUPERT: I will attend him instantly. (*Exit*)

LADY V. (*turning to* DORCAS): And farewell thou. And all of you.

DORCAS: Our hearts go with thee.

LADY V.: And ours stay with you—bruised, but not broken. We are
Vernons still.

SONG.—LADY VERNON.

Queen of the garden bloomed a rose,
    Queen of the roses round her:
Never a wayward wind that blows
    Breathed on the bower that bound her;
The sunset lingered on her face,
    And Phoebus, westward roaming,
Illumined with a golden grace

The empress of the gloaming.
Never a moon at evening rose
    But in the twilight found her
Regal in rest, in red repose,
    Queen of the roses round her!
Into her heart a canker crept,
    Into her soul a sorrow;
Over her head the dew-drops wept,
    "She will be dead to-morrow!"
But still a smile upon her cheek,
    The morrow found her glowing
In crimson state, on all who seek
    Her royal grace bestowing.
Queen of the garden still at noon,
    Queen of the roses round her,
Not until eve the pallid moon
    Dead in the garden found her!

DORCAS and CHORUS: Dead in the garden lay a rose,
    Regal in rest they found her;
ALL: Smiling in death's august repose,
    Queen of the roses round her!

Meanwhile SIR GEORGE *has entered.*
Exeunt DORCAS *and* CHORUS.

DUET.—LADY VERNON and SIR GEORGE.

SIR G.: Alone—alone!
    No friendly tone
   To bid my heart rejoice.
 My son beneath the sighing sea—
 My daughter dear estranged from me!
    No kindly voice
   To say rejoice!
     Alone—alone!
LADY V.: Not whilst I live.
SIR G.: Why kneelest thou to me?
LADY V.: Husband, forgive!
    A suppliant I to thee!
'Twas I who urged our daughter's flight—

Oh! how can I atone?
   Upon that wild and starless night,
      The culprit, I alone!

SIR G.: Then it was thou!

LADY V.: My head I humbly bow.

   SIR GEORGE raises her.

SIR G.: Bride of my youth, wife of my age,
   Who, hand in hand and page by page,
      Hast read life's book with me,
   Upon whose knee our son hath slept,
   Together we have smiled and wept
      Over his grave—the sea.
   Until we quit life's chequered scene,
   Love, let us keep our friendship green;
   Friends we have always, always been,
      Friends let us always be.

LADY V.: Our years are spent, our heads are grey,
   And slowly ebbs the tide away
      That bears us out to sea.

SIR G.: I print a kiss upon thy brow;
   We are too old to quarrel now;
      What have I left but thee?

BOTH: Until we quit life's chequered scene,
   Love, let us keep our friendship green;
   Friends we have always, always been,
      Friends let us always be!

Exeunt.

Re-enter RUPERT.

RUPERT: Methought it good taste not to interrupt them, albeit they
   delay their departure unduly. Sooth to say, the position of my poor
   cousins is pathetic enough, but it behoves them to accept their lot
   with philosophy—as I do.

Enter DORCAS *excitedly, followed by* CHORUS.

RUPERT: How now? How now? Is it so that ye enter our presence?

SCENE.

DORCAS: In frill and feather spic and span,
   A gallant is asking for thee;

I told him to go,
But he wouldn't take "no"—
Oh, he is such a nice young man!
NANCE, GERTRUDE, DEBORAH: We told him to go, etc.
RUPERT: Oh yes, I know that nice young man
He travels in coffee and tea;
And if you're not in,
Leaves behind him a tin
Or a packet of bad Bohea.
CHORUS: Oh, we all of us know, etc.
DORCAS: Oh, sir, he's such a handsome youth!
The nicest I ever did see!
To tell thee the truth
I have never seen youth,
Who was quite such a youth as he!
Exit DORCAS.
NANCE, GERTRUDE, DEBORAH: To tell thee the truth, etc.
RUPERT: Oh yes, I know this self-same youth!
He dabbles a bit in the arts;
He wants you to hire
What you'll never require,
In a series of monthly parts.
CHORUS: He's partial to hours both dark and late,
He has a quick eye for the spoons,
And long will he wait
With his foot in the gate,
In the dusk of the afternoons.
Flourish. Re-enter DORCAS *with* OSWALD *in uniform. He salutes and gives a parchment to* RUPERT.
OSWALD: Good General Monk, with others therein named,
Hath entered London and the King proclaimed.
And by his order I am here to claim
This ancient manor, in King Charles's name!
Dost thou surrender?
RUPERT: Nothing! I have said!
OSWALD: So be it, sire; thy blood be on thy head!
Salutes and exit.
RUPERT: Summon my bodyguard! I fear me, friends,
Some evil to my person this portends.

Enter Puritans, *one by one, loafing, with their hands in their pockets.*

Rupert: Why this disorder? this rebellious mien?

    Where are your books? and why are ye so clean?

Puritans: Bother our books!

        We all intend

        Our evil looks

          And ways to mend.

   We mean to do just what we like,

   So we have all come out on strike.

        Eight hours we'll moan—

          Eight hours we'll sigh—

        Eight hours we'll groan—

          Eight hours we'll pry—

Simeon: But for sixteen we will be free!

Puritans: And so say I!

Chorus: And so say we!

Chorus *fling down their books.*

Dorcas: We have thought the matter out

   And we know what we're about,

      And whatever thou mayst do or say,

   We intend to sing in chorus

   With the gallants who adore us,

      And to merry-make the livelong day!

Chorus: Singing, Tra, la, la, la, la, etc.

Rupert: To a word of warning hark,

   Ere you recklessly embark

      On an undertaking so inane

   As to dedicate to Cupid

   That particularly stupid

      And peculiarly weak refrain

Chorus: Known as Tra, la, la, la, la, etc.

Puritans: From the point of view of wit,

   We are open to admit

      It's a silly sort of thing to say;

   But when musically treated

   And sufficiently repeated,

      It's effective in its simple way.

Chorus: So, sing, Tra, la, la, la, la, etc.

Dance.

Rupert: So, the professional agitator hath been at work here. I must take counsel with McCrankie. His uncompromising puritanism will no doubt find a way out of the difficulty.

Enter McCrankie, *in breeches.*

Rupert: Odds truth! what means this metamorphosis. (Chorus *gather round*)

McCran: Aweel, aweel, I'll tell ye a' aboot it. I wasna tat weel last nicht, and sae, tae warm my heart, I jist had—

Rupert: A wee drappie?

McCran: Wha tauld thee, mon? Sickerly! I had ane wee drappie.

Chorus: He had one wee drappie!

McCran: But somegate I felt waur instead o' better; and sae—weel, I jist had anither wee drappie.

Rupert: He had two wee drappies!

McCran: But twa wee drappies didna reach the cause.

Rupert: So thou hadst three? (McCrankie *shakes his head*)

Dorcas: Four?

Gertrude: Five?

Nance: Six?

McCran: Weel, I didna jistly coont.

Rupert: Well, thou wert past arithmetic; what then?

McCran: I'd a fa'an asleep; an' i' my sleep, got crackin' tae mysel'. An' what dae ye think I said?

Rupert: Mon, I neither ken nor care. (*Exit*)

Song.—McCrankie.

Hech, mon! hech, mon! it gars me greet
    Tae see thy capers mony,
When nature made the earth sae sweet,
    An' life micht be sae bonny.
Why nae accept what fortune sen's
An' learn that earth an' heaven are frien's?
      Eneugh o' hanky-panky—
        Gie ower thy freaks
        An' don the breeks,
      An' be a mon, McCrankie!

CHORUS: Thou'st got 'em on!
McCRANKIE (*proudly*): I've got 'em on!
CHORUS: Thou'st got 'em on, McCrankie!
    At first I thoucht the sudden swap
        Was jist a wee bit risky;
    But noo they're fastened o' the tap
        I feel quite young an' frisky.
    Tae show ye jist the sort o' thing,
    I'm gaun tae dance a Heeland fling,
        An' if ye'll help, I'll thank'ee.
        A wee bit skirl—
        A wee bit whirl—
        A fling wi' auld McCrankie!
CHORUS: A wee bit skirl—
McCRANKIE: A wee bit whirl—
CHORUS: A fling wi' auld McCrankie!

SCOTTISH DANCE.

FINALE OF ACT III.

Cannonade off.
OMNES: Hark! the cannon! Where to hide us?
        Hark! again the trumpet's call!
    Friend afar and foe beside us,
        Death confronts us one and all!
Cannonade.
The door is broken open. Enter MANNERS, *attended by* OSWALD *and others.*
Re-enter SIR GEORGE *and* LADY VERNON.
MANNERS: God save the King!
        These from his hand I bring!
        Gives a warrant to SIR GEORGE.
    Time there was, Sir Knight, thou spurned me from thy gate;
    For my revenge I had not long to wait.
    Thee, in King Charles's name, I re-instal
    The lord of Haddon and of Haddon's Hall.
CHORUS: God save the King!
    God save the King!
LADY V.: But who art thou that bring

Tidings so glad?

Sᴉʀ G.: Thy name?

Mᴀɴɴᴇʀs: John Manners.

Sᴉʀ G.: Rutland's son?

Mᴀɴɴᴇʀs: The same.

Sᴉʀ G.: Thou hast done this for me?

Mᴀɴɴᴇʀs: For one who bore thy name.

Goes up and throws open the doors.

Enter Dᴏʀᴏᴛʜʏ, *whom he leads down the steps to* Sᴉʀ Gᴇᴏʀɢᴇ *and* Lᴀᴅʏ Vᴇʀɴᴏɴ.

Cʜᴏʀᴜs: Lo! our mistress! Haddon's pride!

Home the bridegroom brings his bride!

Mᴀɴɴᴇʀs: Another gift, Sir Knight, I bring,

With favours from our greater king

Who rules beyond the grave.

To thee I now present my bride.

A lover, I thy wrath defied;

A son, thy grace I crave.

Dᴏʀᴏᴛʜʏ (*kneeling at* Sᴉʀ Gᴇᴏʀɢᴇ's *feet*):

Oh, father, wilt thou not forgive me now?

Sᴉʀ G.: Arise, beloved! Thou hast kept thy vow.

Lᴀᴅʏ V.: And all things yield to such a love as thine.

Dᴏʀᴏᴛʜʏ: Oh, praise me not; the merit is not mine.

Love breathed a message through the sphere!

I could not but obey;

To all who have the ears to hear

Love breathes it every day.

Now, in the babbling of the brook,

It murmurs to our souls;

Now, through the lightning's fiery fork

Reverberant it rolls.

It echoes through the solemn night,

It rings all nature through;

For ever, in the angels' sight

To thine own heart be true!

Dᴏʀᴏᴛʜʏ, Lᴀᴅʏ V., Mᴀɴɴᴇʀs, Sᴉʀ G.: Though storms uprise

And cloud the skies,

And thorns where roses grew,

Come sun, come snow,

Come weal, come woe,
To thine own heart be true!
ALL: Though storms uprise, etc.

THE END

A Note About the Author

Sydney Grundy (1848–1914) and Arthur Sullivan (1842–1900) were successful collaborators during the late nineteenth century. Grundy attended Owens College where he studied law before he embarked on his theatrical career. Elsewhere, Sullivan was raised in a musical family where he learned to play multiple instruments at an early age. He would go on to produce *H.M.S. Pinafore* (1878) and *The Pirates of Penzance* (1879). Meanwhile, Grundy worked on *A Little Change* (1872), *A Pair of Spectacles* (1889) and *A Village Priest* (1890).

A Note from the Publisher

Spanning many genres, from non-fiction essays to literature classics to children's books and lyric poetry, Mint Edition books showcase the master works of our time in a modern new package. The text is freshly typeset, is clean and easy to read, and features a new note about the author in each volume. Many books also include exclusive new introductory material. Every book boasts a striking new cover, which makes it as appropriate for collecting as it is for gift giving. Mint Edition books are only printed when a reader orders them, so natural resources are not wasted. We're proud that our books are never manufactured in excess and exist only in the exact quantity they need to be read and enjoyed.

bookfinity

Discover more of your favorite classics with Bookfinity™.

- Track your reading with custom book lists.
- Get great book recommendations for your personalized Reader Type.
- Add reviews for your favorite books.
- AND MUCH MORE!

Visit **bookfinity.com** and take the fun Reader Type quiz to get started.

Enjoy our classic and modern companion pairings!

Classic & Modern

www.ingramcontent.com/pod-product-compliance
Lightning Source LLC
Chambersburg PA
CBHW020604030426
42337CB00013B/1209